THE GEORDIE LAFF INN

by

DICK IRWIN

Illustrated by

R. THOMPSON

© I.S.B.N. 0 85983 029 2

1976

Published by FRANK GRAHAM
6 Queen's Terrace, Newcastle upon Tyne, NE2 2PL

Printed by Howe Brothers (Gateshead) Ltd.

GEORDIE AT THE MATCH

It was raining in the uncovered end at Newcastle United's ground and Geordie was getting soaked. Tucker says to Geordie, "Why divn't ye tak your cap oot o' ye pocket?" To which Geordie replied, "Ye dinna think I'm going to sit in the hoose arl neet wi a wet cap on".

Tucker was getting ready to watch Newcastle United. His wife had wanted him to take her to the pictures. Bursting into tears she cried, "I think you think more of Newcastle United than you think of me!" she sobbed. "I think more of Sunderland than I think of ye", says Tucker.

I went to see the manager of one of our local teams which hadn't been doing so well lately. In fact I rang him up first and asked him what time the kick off was. "What time can you make it for Dick?" he said.

When I was eventually shown into his office he was sitting at his desk surrounded by goldfish in bowls. "What's the idea of all the goldfish?" I asked him. "I love them Dick", he said. "They're the only things around here I can watch open their mouths and never ask for a transfer".

It was a bitter cold frosty Saturday afternoon. A frail old lady came to the gates of St. James' Park. "Can I have a word with Supermac?" she says to the man on the gate. "Look mother", says the Gateman, "It's a terrible cold day, why divvent ye gaan hyem, sit by your fire and listen to the game on your radio?" "Alreet", she says, "But will you give this to Supermac?" handing him a paper packet. "Alreet", says the Gateman, "What is it?" "It's a bit of Carbonate of Soda", she says. "I heard on the wireless the poor sowl was kicking with the wind".

Bob Stokoe was a bit worried. He was thinking about buying his team cigarette lighters, they'd been losing so many matches lately. He met Gordon Lee one night. He says, "Gordon, yor teams dein canny just noo, can ye suggest any method of training for my lads?" "Why", says Gordon, "I'll tell ye what I do. Get eleven dustbins, place them in strategic positions and the lads dribble in and oot of the bins—never fails". "I'll try it", says Bob. Three weeks later they met again. "How's the dustbin method working Bob?" says Gordon. "Ne good at aal", says Bob, "Tried it last Tuesday, the dustbins won seven nowt!"

A little boy went to the team manager. "I'd like to join the team, sir", he said. "How old are you son?" said the manager. "Fourteen, sir", said the boy. "Come back and see me in two years", said the manager. A week later the same laddie came back. "Can I join now sir?" he said. "I told you to come back in two years, didn't I?" said the manager. "I knaa ye did", said the boy, "But I've watched the last two games and it's put years on me".

"HE'S LOST HIS VOICE!"

FESTIVE FRIVOLITY

It was New Year's Eve. The bells of St. Nicholas' Cathedral were ringing the old year out and the new year in. Feeling full of goodwill I said to an old man, "Arn't the bells lovely?" "I canna hear ye son, speak up", he says. So I repeated louder, "Arn't the bells lovely?" I then shouted at the top of my voice, "Arn't the bells lovely!" "Sorry son", he says, "I canna hear ye for the noise of those bloody bells!"

Mind I've packed this carol singing lark in. I went out on Xmas Eve. The first house I went to I sang two carols and a tuning fork came through the letter-box.

Mind Xmas' arn't what they used to be when I was young. Things were that hard my dad used to go out in the lane, every Xmas Eve and fire a revolver. Then he'd come in and tell us bairns that Santa Claus had committed suicide.

I love Xmas because of the parties. I remember me owld grandfethor. He had a favourite Xmas trick. He would put a ship into a whisky bottle and then to get the ship out he would drink the whisky. Then he could never remember how he did the trick.

My mother would say to my Dad. "What are you going to buy these bairns for Xmas? Ye've bought them nowt for years!" "Boil them an egg and tell them it's Easter", he'd say.

I can remember hanging my stockings up on Xmas Eve. "I hope ye divvent think Santa 'll fill them", she said. "No", I told her, "But he might darn them".

I remember the Xmas puddings she used to make! The only thing you could eat was the threepenny bits.

I was the only boy in our street with an air gun. It's understandable because I was the only boy in our street. I remember those cold winter nights. We were so poor my father would suck a peppermint, put his tongue out and we would sit round it warming our hands.

I don't know about you but I think Xmas is a money making affair these days. I was in one of these big department stores in Newcastle where there was a Santa Claus with a big bag of toys. The little bairns would give him a ten pence piece. He would dive in his sack and give them a rubbishy Japanese toy that would blow their hands off. One little girl in rags and tatters; no soles to her feet, no roof to her mouth. "Pleathe Santa, could I have a preshent for ten penth?" she said. He took her tenpence, and dives in his bag. "There ye are hinnie, there's a walkie talkee doll for ye, and a pram with chromium handlebars to push it in, a dressing gown and slippers for yor granny; some baccy, a briar pipe, and a bottle of whisky for yor granda; a dance dress and dance shoes for yor big sister; a set of flick knives for yor big brother, so he can knock the bus conductors aboot". She was laden with presents. "Thank you, Santa", she says. "Do I get all this for ten pence?" "Yes pet", he says, "And tell yor muthor te hev me supper ready when I get hyem!"

It was Xmas Eve. Geordie and his marra had been celebrating. It was a clear frosty night so they thought they'd walk home. Passing a big house they stopped to listen to the bairns singing carols at the front door. They were singing:—

"*Hark the herald angels sing*!
Glory to the new-born king."

Geordie turns to Sep and says, "By gox Sep, I've lived thorty year in Throckley; it's the forst time I knew they had a king in *Newburn*!"

The school teacher was asking the class what nationality they thought Santa Claus was. Little Mary says, "Miss, I think he comes from Iceland because he's always wrapped up in furs". "Very good,

Mary", says the teacher. Up spake Jimmie, "Miss I think he's from Lapland, as he always uses reindeers". "Good answer, Jimmie", she says. Up lowps little Geordie. "Please miss, I think Santa must be Irish". "Whatever makes you think that?" said the teacher. "Why miss", says Geordie, "On wor hoose we've got a front door, a back door, and French windows, and the daft fyuel comes doon the chimney".

Tosher Fleck had two little laddies. Horace was a well behaved child, young Geordie was just the opposite, a right worky-ticket. Comes Xmas Eve, Tosher thinks he'll teach Geordie a lesson. He waited till they got to sleep. Then he filled Horace's stocking with good things and little Geordie's stocking he filled with horse manure, or as we call it in Gosforth *fertilizer*. On Xmas morning the two young Flecks were up with the lark. Horace says, "Look what Santa's fetched me, a flashlamp, a transistor, Billy stampers, a football. What's he fetched ye Geordie?" Young Geordie scratching his head said, "He must have fetched me a pony but its hopptit".

Have you ever wondered why you always see a fairy on top of a Xmas tree? Well I'll tell you. A few Xmas' ago Santa had a nasty dose of flu and wished he could go to bed with a whisky and Beecham's, instead of delivering presents. The Xmas fairy said, "Go to bed Santa, I'll yoke the reindeer up and deliver your presents for you". Santa thanked her and went to bed. He'd just got nicely off to sleep when the phone rang. It was the Xmas fairy. "Sorry to bother you Santa", she says, "But I'm in Seaton Burn and I've found a parcel for Jimmy Broon with no address on it. What shall I do?" Santa growled, "Leave it on the Pollis Station steps and divvent bother me ne more!" Two hours later the phone rang again. Santa was raving. It was the fairy again. "What's wrang noo!" yells Santa. "I'm in Dinnington Village now", she says, "I've got a Xmas tree with no address on it, what shall I do?" "How big is it?" says Santa. "It's aboot two foot six", she says. "Ye knaa what ye can de wi that tree!" says Santa.

And that folks is why you *always* see a fairy on *top* of a Xmas tree.

Think it over!

My mother was cleaning the windows one Xmas time when she spotted the dustbin man coming up the path. He emptied the bin, put the lid back on again (first time he'd done that), dusted the lid with his cap and knocked at the front door. When my mother answered the door he said "Good morning, madam, Merry Xmas. I'm the man who empties your dustbin". "I'm pleased to meet you", said my mother. "I'm the woman that fills it".

I'll never forget last Xmas. We bought our little boy a chemistry set for Xmas. On Xmas morning he opened it to see what he could find. I don't know what he found but we are still looking for the roof.

My mate Sep was laughing on Xmas day when I met him in the pub. "Ye look pleased wi yersel", I says. "I am anaal", he replied. "The mother-in-law's been yapping on for a Jaguar for months. I bought her one for Xmas and d'ye knaa what Dick, its bitten her heed off".

Geordie Smith asked his wife what she'd like for Xmas. "An animal skin coat", she said. So Geordie bought her a donkey jacket.

A FEW FISHY STORIES

Geordie was enjoying himself fishing on a bridge in Warkworth. A very posh gent walked by. "Good morning my man", he said. "Have you had any luck?" Geordie says "Any luck! Why d'ye knaa yesterday I caught forty salmon here". "Really!" said the gent, "Do you know who I am?" "No! I divvent", says Geordie. "Well my man! I am the chief magistrate here, and this is my estate". Geordie says, "D'ye knaa whe I am, I'm the biggest liar in Seghill".

Geordie was fishing off the pier at Amble when he got cracking to an American tourist fishing next to him. The yank in typical American braggin said. "Ye know pal back in the States I caught a fish so big

mah buddies wouldn't let me haul it into the boat in case it capsized us". "Funny ye shud say that!" says Geordie. "D'ye knaa the same thing happened to me on the Queen Elizabeth".

Every Sunday morning this mate of mine would go fishing in Blyth. This Sunday he'd been fishing for three hours without a single bite, when he noticed a fellow further along who kept landing big fish, taking them off the hook and throwing them back. After, about twelve times this mate of mine couldn't stand it any longer. He went to this bloke and said, "I've been here all morning, caught nowt, ye've been catching big fish aal the time and hoying them back. Why d'ye do this?" "Why", the fellow says, "It's like this, they're ne good to me, ye see we've only got a smaal frying pan in wor hoose".

I tried fishing mesel once but I soon got fed up. I went to this little pub for a drink where I met this old sailor. After a pint or two he got on about his experiences. "D'ye knaa, son, I was once shipwrecked on a desert island and lived for a week on a tin of sardines!" "By gox!" I says. "Ye hadn't much room to move aboot had ye?"

Geordie and Sep Walker made a bet of £5 that Geordie could catch more fish than Sep. On the following Sunday they went to Blyth Pier with tackle, bait, the lot. Geordie happened to lean over too far, slipped and fell in. Sep pulled him out. "Hi lad!" he says, "If you're ganna dive for them the bet's off".

Dodie Stewart had been made redundant at the pit. Passing through Seahouses he saw a notice on Joe Douglas, the fisherman's window. Shrimpers wanted, good wages for the right men. Dodie thinks, I'll hev a go! The boss says, "I think you'll do". Dodie says, "What do ye pay?" The boss says, "I'll give you union rate £1 an hour". "Champion", says Dodie, "When can I start?" "Ye can start noo", says the boss. "Can I hev a sub?" says Dodie. "Ye'll hev a rowing boat like the rest", says the gaffer.

GEORDIE JUSTICE

Geordie was in the dock. The judge recognised him. "What brought you here?" he asked. "Two pollis' your honour", says Geordie. "Drunk I suppose", said the judge. "That's reet yor honour", says Geordie, "Both of them!"

Geordie's wife Meggie dashed into the Police Station crying. "I want a separation from wor Geordie!" she says. "He's come in drunk and knocked me black and blue. I haven't got a white mark on me body". "I'm afraid you can't get a separation as easy as that, madam", says the Inspector. "Before you can get rid of Geordie he's got to be unfaithful to you". "He's been that an aal!" says Meggie. "D'ye knaa, sir, he's not the father of my last child".

The other day I meets owld Sep Potts. I'd nivor seen him for weeks. "What cheor Sep!" I says, "It's grand to see ye looking so weel. Hev ye been bad?" "No Dick, hinney", he says. "I've been in jail". "Jail!" I says. "What's an old man like ye been dein in jail?" "Why it's like this Dick", he says. "I was oot for a waak the other day when a young pollis pulls me up. 'We're one man short at an identification parade, would you like to help out?' he asks. Why I had nowt te de so I went. Well when we got to the Police Station they stood me in a row with aboot ten other criminals. Then they shone some spotlights on us, when this young dolly bird in a mini-skirt walked in. She stopped in front of me, pointed her finger at me, and said 'That's him! That's the dirty owld man who dragged me up a lane and assaulted me!' Why Dick hinney", says Sep, "I was so proud I pleaded guilty".

Geordie was in court charged with molesting a young milkmaid. "I think", said the judge, "We will hear this case in camera". "What's that?" says Geordie. "Never you mind my man!" said the judge. "The defence knows what it is. It doesn't concern you. Carry on with the case". During the trial the Judge says to Geordie, "What happened?" "Why yor honour", says Geordie, "I took Mary to the pictures, on the way back we waalked ower a field. We stopped under a tree, had a bit kiss, a bit cuddle, and then we had a bit la-de-daa". "Stop!" said the Judge, "What the devil is La-de-daa?" "Well yor honour", says Geordie, "The defendant knaas waat it is, the prosecution knaas what it is, the jury knaas waat it is, and if ye'd had yor bloody camera there ye'd've knaan anaal!"

Bantie Johnson and Tucker Stewart decided to join the Police Force seeing that the pit was closing down and they'd be redundant. When they arrived for the interview Tucker says to Bantie, "Ye gaan in forst, then ye can put me wise to the questions". Why Bantie gaans in first, and the Sargeant says to him, "So you wish to join the force?" "That's reet", says Bantie. "Well I'll start by asking you", says the Sargeant, "Who killed our Lord?" "I divvent knaa", says Bantie. "I'll give you a week to find out", says the Sargeant. On the way out Tucker says, "Howay Bantie, what did he ask ye?" "I'll tell ye later", says Bantie, "Divvent stop us noo, I'm on a murder case!"

All my family had funny ends. My uncle Peter was a painter. He fell out of bed, he had a matt-finish. My uncle Frank was a French polisher. He swallowed a bottle of shellac. He had a terrible death but a lovely finish. My grandfather had the worst end of the lot. They hung him. He drowned my granny in bed. He shoved her through the mattress and she landed in the spring.

I'll never forget the day they hung me granda. One cold frosty December morning they took him in the Prison yard at Durham Prison. The hangman was a canny fellow. He says te me Grandad "Would ye like a cigarette?" "No thanks son", he says, "I'm trying to chuck it". "Well have you any last request?" "I hev anaal", he says, "Keep yor trap shut".

Magistrate to Police Constable. "What made you think the prisoner in the dock was under the influence of drink?" "Well yor honour", says the Pollis, "He put twopence through the letter-box, rang the front door bell, put an empty milk bottle to his ear, said 'Ne reply', then went to sleep on the doorstep!"

Another mate of mine got in trouble, so he emigrated to South Africa. Got a job in a gold mine. He finished up in court. They caught him pinching lead off the roof.

The Magistrate was remonstrating with Geordie, on a shop-breaking charge. "I don't understand this case!" he said. "It appears you took all the articles off the counter, yet left all the money in the till undisturbed. Why did you do this?" "Look, yur honour", says Geordie, "Divvent ye start on that, wor lass' been on to me summick awful aboot it".

Geordie was in Durham for poaching. Checking his kit he discovered his long johns, shaving brush and razor were missing. He says to the screw, "I demand an interview with the Governor!" He was ushered in to the Governor's office. "Well my man", said the Governor, "What is your complaint?" "Why sir", says Geordie, "I think ye should knaa this. Ye've got a thief in this prison!"

Three men in the Dock. Judge to first man, "Where do you live?" 35 Acacia Avenue, your honour". Judge to second man, "Where do you live?" Second man, "No fixed abode your honour". Judge to third man, "And you my man?" "Your honour", says number three, "I've got a room off him".

This character was in court on a charge of stealing ten bottles of 'Brown Ale'. "So you stole ten bottles of 'Brown Ale'?" said the Judge. "That's reet, yor honour", says Geordie. "Well!" said the judge, "Go back and steal another two and we'll make a case of it".

A little boy was crying his eyes out in the street when a kindly policeman asked him, "What are you crying for son?" "I'm looking for my daddy", sobbed the boy. "What's your daddy like?" said the pollis. "He likes beer, football and women", said the little laddie.

MEDICAL MIRTH

I wasn't feeling ower grand so I thowt I'd gaan and see the doctor. On the way I meets Sep Walker. "Where are ye off te Dick?" "I'm away to see the doctor", I tells him. "Which doctor", says Sep. "No!" I tells him, "He's a white man".

Half way up the Stairs I meets a fellow coming down with a face like a fiddle. "What's wrang wi ye?" I asks him. "I've just seen the doctor and seys I've got three days to live!" "Cheer up", I says, "It'll soon gaan ower".

When I gets in the Surgery it was choc-a-bloc and ye knaa how it is, ye get interested in them magazines, 'Queen Victoria pregnant, look what that ice-berg did to the Titanic', and when you're not looking they pinch yor turn. I boxed clever, I sat next to a fellow with a chopping axe in his head.

When I eventually got in to see the doctor I says to him, "How do I stand doc?" "It beats me!" he said, "Sit doon. What's your trouble anyhow?" I says, "I've been eating a lot of grapes lately". "Grapes!" he said, "They won't harm you!" "These ones will", I said, "They're off the wallpaper".

"Behind the screen", he said. "Take your clothes off!" I did, ye feel daft, nowhere to put your hands. "Go back!" he says, "Take your socks off!" "I've got them off!" I says. "By God your feet are dirty", he said. "Naturally", I replied, "I'm older than you".

He took me to a little room with a shelf about 10 feet high, full of little wine glasses. "I want you to fill one of these", he says. "What!" I says, "From here?" Well he gave me a good examination. "I can't see much wrong with you", he says. "I think you've got a touch of Alice". "What's Alice?" I says. "I don't know", he said, "But Christopher Robin went down with it.

Mind ye meet some funny folk at the doctors. A bloke came in one day. The doctor examined him. "Have you got a pain that starts at the base of your left shoulder, that works its way to the pit of your stomach?" "Yes doctor, that's exactly my symptoms", said the chap. "That's funny", said the doctor, "I've got the same, I wonder what it is".

But there was more to come. A kipper came into the Surgery. *A kipper*. It said to the doctor, "They tell me smokings bad for you". "That's right", said the doctor. "That's funny", said the kipper, "It cured me".

If I live to be twenty seven I shall never forget one day. A big Zulu walked into the Doctor's Surgery with a parrot on his head. The parrot looked at the doctor and said, "Can you take this blackhead off my foot?"

Geordie had to be taken in to hospital for an operation. When they had got him nicely tucked in bed the pretty nurse said, "There you are, Mr. Smith, you can have a bottle whenever you wish". "Thanks vary much hinney", says Geordie, "There's twenty pence, get one for yorsel".

Half an hour later the matron came to Geordie's bedside. "Mr. Smith", she said, "You have made one mistake in the admission form you filled in. You've got height five feet six inches—That's right. You've got religion C. of E.—That's right. But where it says sex, you've put 'Not very often'—It should have been male".

Next morning the doctor came round the ward with students. He stopped at Geordie's bed. "A simple case of Hernia", he explained.

"Stand up my man". He put his hand on Geordie's hernia and said, "Cough!" Geordie thought he said 'Off' and made a run for it. When they got him back in bed the doctor said, "Tomorrow you are going to the Theatre". "Good", says Geordie, "I hope there's a canny show on". "Don't worry", said the surgeon, "I guarantee you'll be in stitches when you come out of this one".

Then there was Tucker Johnston—he said to his Doctor, "Can you give me something for the wind?" The doctor gave him a kite! Nearly as bad as my G.P. I asked him if he could give me something for my liver. He gave me a pound of onions.

There were a few strange cases in Geordie's ward. A fellow next to him had matrimonial thrombosis—he married a clot. A seaman farther down had alcoholic constipation—he couldn't pass a pub.. But the funniest was a coloured man beside Geordie. 9 a.m. the nurse got him up. "Your enema", she said. Ten minutes later the matron came to him. "Enema", she said. Twenty minutes later the doctor came. Same thing, "Enema". When the staff went in the office the nurse said, "I've just given that coloured gentleman his enema". "Good heavens!" said the matron, "I gave him one as well!" "So did I!" said the doctor. "We'd better go and see how he is". When they got to his bed it was empty. "Have you seen that coloured gentleman?"

they asked Geordie. "Aye!" said Geordie, "He went alang te the netty hole an hour ago!" They went along knocking on all the toilet doors. When they knocked on the fifth door a little voice said, "Who goes dere; friend or enema?"

Passing the Princess Mary Maternity Hospital I noticed this young man pacing up and down, wringing his hands and looking very nervous. I thought I'd console him. "Is she in there?" I asked him. "Yes", he replied. "Don't worry", I said, "My mates wife has been in there seven times, no bother". "That's aal varry weel", he said, "But this is gan t' ruin my honeymoon".

Talking aboot Maternity Hospitals; they've got a special waiting room for expecting fathers. There was a Scotsman, Irishman and Geordie waiting when the nurse came out with a little baby in her arms as black as the back of a fireplace. Jock looked at it. "It's no mine!" he said. "Bejabers! it's not mine either", says Paddy. Geordie took one look and said, "It'll be mine, she burns everything she makes".

An apple a day keeps the doctor away, so the old saying goes. That's why the fellow who eloped with the doctor's wife took ten stone of apples with him.

The doctor told Malcolm Sadler he'd have to go through an operation. "Will I be able to play the piano after the operation?" he asked the doctor. "I don't see why not", the doctor replied. "That's champion!" said Malcolm, "I couldn't play it before".

Old farmer White was 97 years old. He took unto himself a bride of 25 years of age. Worried about age disparity he consulted his doctor for advice. The doctor said, "Well John, there is a big age gap. My advice to you is take in a lodger". A few months later the doctor met the farmer at the Cattle Mart. "Now John", he said, "You're looking well. How's the wife?" "Oh she's grand doctor, she's expecting ye knaa!" "Good", says the doc, "How's the lodger?" "Oh!" says Old John, "She's expecting anaal".

Mrs. Thompson was worried. She rang the doctor. "My six year old boy has swallowed a fountain pen". "Sorry!" said the doctor, "I won't be able to come round for three to four hours. I've a few patients to visit". "Oh doctor!" she said, "What can I do in the meantime?" "Well", said the doctor, "You'll just have to use a pencil! Won't you?"

Geordie was off colour. The doctor examined him, later he said to Geordie's wife, "Your husband must have peace and quiet. Here is a very strong sleeping powder". "When do I give it to him, doctor?" says Liz. "You don't", said the doctor, "You take it yourself".

GEORDIE ON THE BEER

Ye meet aal sorts in wor Geordie pubs. A bloke in the 'Blacksmith's Arms' says to the barmaid, "Can I hev a pint of 1914 beer, pet?" The barmaid was dubious and consulted the manager. "There's a bloke in the bar, must be barmy", she says. "He's asking for a pint of 1914 beer". "Just give him a pint of Best Scotch", says the boss, "He'll never know the difference". The barmaid filled a pint of Best Scotch. "There you are, sir", she said, "One pint of 1914 beer". "Thanks hinney!" says our friend, "There's fourpence".

I was in this pub on Xmas Eve. A bloke next to me kept ordering two whiskys. He would drink one and pour the other one in his waistcoat pocket. After about seven repetitions of this the barman got curious. "Excuse me sir", he said, "Why do you keep drinking one whisky and pouring the other in your waistcoat pocket?" "Thash my business!" says the man, "Ish my money, I'll do what I like, and if ye divvent shut up I'll give ye a bat in the gob!" Just then a little mouse stuck its head out of his waistcoat pocket, sparred up and squeaked, "And that goes for your bloody cat an aal!"

The bar was full in the Duke of Wellington. A man with a huge Great Dane walked in. "Ye'll hev te get that dog oot of here", says the landlord. "It might upset the tables!" The man took his dog out and tied it to a lamp post. Later a bloke comes in the bar. "Has anybody got a Great Dane fastened to a lamp post here?" "Yes I have", says the first man, "Why?" "I'm sorry to tell you", says the second man, "It's deed!" "What killed it?" says the first man. "My dog did", says the second man. "What sort of dog is yours?" "A Chihuahua". "How could your little dog kill my huge Great Dane?" asks the first man. "It stuck in its throat" replied the second man.

I walked into this little country hotel and ordered a drink. "Cheers!" I said to mine host, "I must compliment you on your bar, real olde world, spitoons and sawdust on the floor". "Sawdust!" says the manager, "You should have been here last night, before the fight, that was furniture!" "I'll have to watch my P's and Q's", I said. "You'll have to watch your hat and coat", he says. I was watching my hat and coat when somebody pinched my beer.

Needless to say I got out of there sharpish. The next pub I went in was called the Bee Hive. They called it the Bee Hive cos everyone that went in got stung. The first thing I saw as I passed through the swing doors was one of the local beauties, resplendent in her traditional Northumbrian costume, cloth cap, clay pipe, hob-nail boots, varicose veins, warts, pimples, the lot. She looked lovely. "Are you going to have one?" I asked her. "No hinney, it's the way me coats fastened", she said. "You don't understand", I replied, "Will ye hev a drink?" "I'll hev a large port", she said. So I gave her a photograph of Southampton docks.

I strolled into the back singing room of the Bee-Hive. They had one of those singing piano players there (they've got them in all the colliery pubs), the Russ Conway of Seghill sitting at the Beckstein working himself, singing and playing, "Let me go—ouch, Let me go—ouch". I thought, 'What the hell's the matter wi him'. I found out! The dart board was hanging on his back.

Tucker had just come back from holiday at Blackpool and was telling Geordie how he got a glass of whisky for nowt. "I went in this pub", he said, "Where they had a monkey on the counter. I ordered a whisky, and when the manager wasn't looking I picked the monkey up and hoyed it out the window. When the manager asked what was the trouble I said that monkey drank my whisky so I hoyed it oot the window. The manager apologised and filled my glass again". Two weeks later Geordie walked into a pub in Tynemouth. Lo and behold there was a monkey on the counter. Here goes, he thought. He orders a double brandy, waited till the manager's back was turned, picks the monkey up, crash, straight through the window. Up storms the manager, "What's gannin on here?" he says. "Why", says Geordie, "That monkey supped me brandy, so I hoyed it oot the window". "Is that so?" said the manager, "It would have a hell of a job, it's been stuffed for the last ten years".

Geodies wife, Liz, was complaining to her next door neighbour, Mrs. Hogarth, about Geordie's drinking habits. "I've brayed him, knocked him black and blue, but it's made nee difference. He's just as bad". "D'ye knaa" says Annie, "Wor Tom was the same, but I cured him. I just treated him with kindness". "I'll try that", says Liz. That night Geordie staggers in, palatic as usual. Liz had a nice supper ready, she sat him in the armchair in front of a blazing fire; took his shoes off, put his slippers on, filled his pipe and lit it for him. After supper she says, "Well Pet, I think we'll gan te bed noo, eh?" "Aye, we might as weel", says Geordie, "The wife'll just murder us, if I gaan hyem noo!"

Three members of the hunting, shooting, fishing fraternity were drinking in the lounge of the 'Eldon'. One remarked to the other, "You know James, it takes all kinds to make a world. Take these big daft pitmen from Bedlington, haven't got the brains they were born with". A big fella with cloth cap and muffler came across. "I heerd what ye said, noo I'm a pitman, I'm from Bedlington and I take offence. I've a mind to knock yor block off!" "We wer'nt alluding to you old man", said one toff, "Have a drink, have a cigar". Two hours later they were still regaling him with drinks when the pitman says, "I've missed the bus noo, I'll hev to waalk hyem". "Not at all old man", they said. "Come home, stay with us and we'll run you home tomorrow". They took him to a big mansion in Rye Hill, wined and dined him and offered him a bed in the children's room or a couch in front of the fire in the living room. Not wanting to disturb the bairns he chose the sofa. Next morning he woke to see a smashing dolly bird in a mini skirt lighting the fire. "Morning pet", he says, "You're a bonny lass, who are you?" "I'm the maid sir", she said. "I sleep in the children's room. Who are you?" "Me!" he says, "I'm one of those big daft pitmen from Bedlington".

Geordie had been gazing on the wine when it was red, on the bus going home. He was singing 'Blaydon Races' when a lady rebuked him. "My man!" she said, "You are a disgrace to your sex". "You're the ugliest woman I've seen in my life", says Geordie, "And you are the drunkenest lout I've ever met!" she said. "Mebbe!" says Geordie, "But I'll be sober tomorrow".

One of the strangest characters I ever met in a pub was a little fellow who kept ordering pints and paying for them with a bit of boody, (pieces of china ware). His mate explained to the bar tender, "He's a bit queer, just humour him or he may get violent; I'll square you up at closing time". Well at closing time the barman duly totted up the cost and said to the little fellow's mate, "I've counted the bits of 'boody' and the total comes to three pound ten shillings". "That's O.K.", says his mate, "Can you change a dustbin lid?"

If here aint Missus's poor Old Cat!-what a treat them ere Tetotalers must have had!

T was a "Tippler," uncommonly ill.

The landlord of the 'Trafagar' was worried, his custom was falling off, and he was telling me it was all due to *mice*. "Dick", he says, "The place is wick with them. They're running ower the floor, up the walls and ower the ceiling. I've tried everything. No results". "Have you tried stuffing broken glass in their holes?" I asked him. "Nee good man, Dick", he said, "I canna catch them".

Sammy Jarrat had a stroke of luck the other night. He won a raffle in the local. The prize was a bottle with 200 shillings in it. He celebrated with a few broon ales. Carrying the bottle up the front path and putting the key in his door the bottle slipped and broke. Shillings were all over the path. 'Oh', he thinks, 'I'll leave them till the morning, neebody 'll see them in the dark'. Next morning his wife woke him up. "Guess what I found on the doorstep", she says. "I knaa", says Sammy, "200 shillings". "No!" she says, "100 bottles of milk".

Jimmy Mason was drinking in the bar when one of his mates said, "Jim! I think there's something you should knaa; as soon as ye come oot for a pint there's a bloke drives up to your hoose in a white Cortina, and visits yor lass. In fact he might be at yor hoose noo!" Jimmy dashed home; he lived in a high-rise flat. Up the lift, 20th floor. Their lass is standing in the kitchen when Jimmy burst in. "Where is he? I'll morder him!" "Where's who?" she says. "Ye knaa fine!" he shouts, "Ye've got a bloke hidden here". "There's nebody here", she says. Just then Jimmy hears a car start, and looking out of the window he sees a white Cortina pulling away. Quick as a flash Jim picks up the fridge, throws it out the window, straight through the roof of the car! Their lass picks up the rolling pin and belts Jim over the nut. Jim wakes up in hospital, all bandages. There's a chap in the next bed, all plaster. "What happened to you mate?" asked Jim. "Why I'm a commercial traveller", says this bloke, "My last call, just moving off, when some idiot throws a fridge out of a window, straight through my car roof". In the bed was a little bloke, all bandaged, legs in traction. Jim says, "Ye look to have had a rough time son, what happened to you?" "Ye'll not believe this", says the little bloke, "I was sitting in this fridge . . .".

It's not the world we live in hinney, it's the folk that live in it, that's what makes life unbearable. Ye'll nivvor guess who I met in the lounge of 'The Three Mile' the other neet, Maggie Thatcher. By what a canny lass, taalks a bit swanky mind. She went to a High School—Matthew Bank. She stood me a pint and said, "Richard, we must wage war on poverty". I says, "Maggie hinney, your reet". I went strite oot and shot a tramp.

I was talking to another lady—had a glass eye. I didn't know, it just came out in the conversation.

Another lady had an unusual dog. "What sort of a dog is that missis?" I asks her. "That sir, happens to be a Mexican Spit" "That's funny", I said, "I've never seen a Mexican spit". Whereupon the little dog looked at me, said "Senor!" And spit right in my eye.

Bill Smith was putting on weight. His mate met him in the boozer. "Why divvent ye gaan to one of them Sauna Steam Baths, there's one alang the road? The fat'll drop off ye like snow off a dyke". After a pint or two Bill decided to try the Sauna Bath. On the way back he saw this place full of steam. "This'll be it", he says, so he walks in, takes his clothes off, and felt a right Charlie. He was in a fish and chip shop.

MIXED GRILL

Tucker met Geordie one day. "By lad", he says, "My luck's reet oot just noo". "How's that?" says Geordie. "Why", says Tucker, "I've just lost a packet on the horses, I've had me car pinched and me little laddie's broken his leg. Howse that for bad luck?" "That's nowt!" says Geordie, "I bowt a suit with three pair of troosers. Two days later I burnt a hole in the jacket pocket".

I met my owld mate Jonty in the street. "How's Jonty?" I says, "D'ye fancy a pint?" "No thanks Dick hinney", he says, "I've joined Byker Mission, I've given it up, in fact I've been reborn". "Reborn, hev ye noo!" I says, "Why ye've still got them bandy legs, I think I'd hev changed them.

Geordie was walking towards the Brough Park Dog Stadium. Crowds of people were coming towards him. He says to an old woman, "Is that the Dogs coming oot hinney?" "No mistor!" she says, "It's the mugs coming oot, the dogs are still inside".

Then there was this other Geordie who was a horse racing fanatic. His wife got fed up, "Horses! Horses!" she says, "Ye canna remember a single thing unless it's connected with horses! I bet ye divvent even knaa what day we got married on?" "Sartinly I can", says Geordie, "It was the Saturday after Windsor Lad won the Derby".

Tommy Dodds won the pools and bought a big new hoose. He was showing me aroond it. He took me in the tiled bathroom, opened the window and shouted, '*Green Side Up*'. Then we went into bedrooms.

Same thing. Opened windows and shouted '*Green Side Up*'. Same in Living room, lounge and kitchenette, opened windows and shouted, '*Green Side Up*'. When we'd completed tour he says, "Well Dick, what do you think of the house?" "Varry nice Tom", I says, "But why do you keep shouting '*Green Side Up*' oot the windows?" "Why it's like this Dick", he says, "I've got two Irishmen laying the lawn".

The shipyards were idle so Geordie gets a job as a rent man, collecting rents up Rye Hill area. He knocks at one door and a great big Pakistani fellow opens the door brandishing a hayfork. Geordie turned and ran. When he got back to Head Office he says to his boss, "I'm packing this job in. A big Pakistani attacked me with a hayfork". "He musn't have been feeling too good", says the boss. "Give it another go". So Geordie goes the next day, same house, same Pakistani gent. All smiles, paid the rent on the dot. "By! what a difference to yesterday", says Geordie, "Ye went for me with a hayfork". "No need to worry", said the Pakistani, "I was making the beds".

Joe Robson was celebrating his 25th Wedding Anniversary and he says to his wife Phoebe. "Is there owt ye'd like for a present, pet?" She says, "I'd love a bath in champagne". So Joe goes and buys 25 bottles of champagne and teams them in the bath. "There ye are", he says to her, "It's all yours". As soon as she'd finished Joe was upstairs with the empty bottles, a ladle and a funnel. He filled 25 bottles, and there was still one left. He turned to Phoebe and said, "Oh no! Ye didn't, did ye?"

Willie Gardner went to London to watch United play at Wembley. He booked into a London hotel and was just signing the register when he threw the pen down. "I'm not staying here lad!" he says to the receptionist, "I've just seen a flea on the register". "I'm sorry sir", she said, "But you must understand there are fleas in even the best hotels". "I knaa that", says Willie, "But it's the only hotel I've been in where they jump on the book to see which room you're staying in!"

Noo here's a couple of shipyard stories:—

An American millionaire was over here visiting Swan Hunter's. He pulled up a riveter, "I say Bud, can you tell me where the urinal is?" "What colour is her funnels?" said the riveter.

A party of Japanese business men visited the Naval Yard. When they arrived back in Japan they were summoned before the Emperor who asked them their impression of Geordieland. "Your illustrious highness", said one Japanese, "I was amazed, the natives of Tyneside speak fluent Japanese. I was inspecting a ship in Walker Naval Yard, when I distinctly heard one workman say to another, HIMATE—HOYA HAMMER HOWER HERE".

Geordie had been in action at the front for two years without a spot of leave, but his wife Bella sent him £2 a week without fail. Then one lucky day his name came on the board for leave. It was two in the morning and pelting down with rain when he arrived home in Seghill. He walked up the front path and knocked at the front door. When the door opened there was a big Yank in pyjamas. He looked at Geordie and said, "Say bud, who are you?" "I'm the husband here!" says Geordie, "Who the hell are ye?" "I'm the guy whose been sending you those lil ole £2 every week", says the yank.

"Are ye noo", says Geordie, "Look son, ye'd better get back te bed as sharp as ye can, ye'll get your death of cold standing here ın this weather".

They say truth is stanger than fiction. Years ago my cousin and his mate worked in the pits in their teens beside an old man who was a proper old grouse. So one day they decided to play a trick on him. They waited till he was having a break away from where he was working and unharnessed the pony from the tub, turned the pony round facing the tub and harnessed it up again. Then they hid to see how the old man reacted when he came back. He looked at the pony in surprise, walked around it, one hand on hip, the other scratching his head and shouted, "Yiv cowped yor bloody creels in lad! Noo ye can coup yer bloody creels oot again!"

I went to see my Granny the other say: she was in a terrible state. "Dickie hinny", she says, "Ye'll hev to hev a word with that man ower the road. D'ye knaa I can stand at the window and see that man undressing. Ye'll have to taalk tiv im about it". I looked out the window, "Why, Granny", I says, "You're making a lot of noise about nowt. I canna see a thing from here". "I knaa", she says, "But just ye stand on that table".

This fellow standing next to me had seventeen pints lined up on the bar counter. He kept taking a quick drink from each glass in turn. I thought he must be a nutter. "Why d'ye keep doing that?" I asked him. "Why Dick", he says, "I've been like this since I had my accident". "Oh, did you have an accident?" I asked him. "I did anaal", he said, "I once had one knocked over".

The anti-drink temperance preacher was doing his stuff on the Quayside one Sunday morning. "My friends", he says, "Strong drink and alcohol are evil things and I shall prove it. Look at the happy marriages, homes and families that have been wrecked through strong drink". A voice came from the back of the crowd, "Aye, and look at the ships that hev been wrecked through watter!"

Geordie Broon had a plague of black beetles. He read in a book that a hedgehog was the cure. On Saturday he went to the match. After a few pints he decided to buy a hedgehog. After buying it he asked what was the best to feed it on. "Greens", said the man, "Cabbage leaves, lettuce, shamrock, when it's in season". So Geordie buys cabbage and lettuce but the thing wouldn't look at them. Geordie thinks, 'I've bowt a dud!' So he takes it to the R.S.P.C.A. He says to the vet, "I've bowt a hedgehog, but it refuses to eat". The vet took it in the surgery to examine it. When he returned he said to Geordie, "Do you drink, sir?" "Aye", says Geordie, "Nowt but Newcastle Broon Ale". "I thought so", said the vet, "This is not a hedgehog you've bought; it's a lavatory brush".

A TYNESIDE MOTHERS LETTER TO HER SON

Dear Son

Just a few lines to let you know I'm still alive. I'm writing this letter slowly cos I know you can't read very fast. You won't know the house when you come home—we've moved. About your father, he's got a lovely new job, he has about 500 men under him. He's cutting the grass in the cemetery. There was a washing machine in the new house when we moved in. But it's not working too good. Last week I put fourteen shirts into it, pulled the chain, and haven't seen them since. Your sister Mary had a baby this morning, but I haven't found out whether it's a boy or girl yet, so I don't know if you're an uncle or an aunt. Your uncle Mick drowned last week in a vat of whisky at Newcastle Breweries. Some of his workmates dived in to save him, but he fought them off bravely. We cremated his body and it took three days for the fire to go out. Your father didn't have much to drink at Xmas. I put a bottle of castor oil in his Brown Ale. It kept him going till New Year's Day. I went to the doctor on Thursday, your father came with me. The doctor put a small glass tube in my mouth and told me not to open it for ten minutes. Your father offered to buy it off him. It only rained twice last week; first for three days, then for four days. Monday was so windy that one of the chickens laid the same egg four times. We had a letter from the undertaker, he says if we don't pay the last instalment on your Granny—up she comes.

That's all for now.

P.S. I was going to send you £10, but I'd already sealed the letter.

Love

Mother

"I told you he was a Big Dart Player!"

Talking about Irishmen. I was in a club one night and a ventriloquist came on stage with his doll. Very good he was. Halfway through his act he started cracking Irish gags. A big fellow in the audience jumped up and shouted, "Oim an Irishman and oi take offence at you fellows taking the mickey out of the Oirish, and oive a mind to punch your nose!" "I'm very sorry", said the ventriloquist, "If I've offended you, I humbly apologise. It was not intended. I beg your pardon". "Oh you're alright", said the Irishman, "It's that little Spaldeen on your knee oim on aboot".

When I was a lad we had a butcher in my town who was an avid Newcastle United supporter. Every Saturday he would close his shop, hang his apron up, don his black and white scarf and away to the match. One Saturday he was just closing up when old Mrs. Fleck walked into the shop. She'll taalk me heed off, he thinks, and I'll miss the game. "Hev ye got such a thing as a chicken Mr. Rochester?" she says. "I've got company coming on Sunday". He went into the back-shop, he had only one chicken left. "How's that?" he says, hoying it on the counter, "Fifteen shillings". "Why!" says aald Mrs. Fleck,

"Thanks Mate, That's yours with the Black Speckles!"

"It's a bit small hinney, hev ye got nowt bigger?" He goes into the back-shop again, stretched its legs, blew it up with a bicycle pump, hoys it on the counter again. "How's that?" he says, "One pound". "That's better", she says, "Tell ye what, I'll take the two".

Aad Tot and aad Willie were keen bowl players. Aad Willie says to Tot, "I wonder if there's any bowling greens in heaven". "I'll tell you wat", says Tot, "The forst one of us to snuff it will come back and tell the other". Why a fortnight later aad Willie kicks the bucket. Tot's just bowling his wood when he felt a tap on his shoulder. There was aad Willie behind him. "I towld ye I'd come back and let ye knaa Tot", he says. "Why I've got some good news for ye, and some bad news anaal. But foirst the good news. Ye've got nowt te worry aboot regarding bowling greens in Heaven. The place is full of them and ye can play to your hearts content". "Champion!" says Tot, "And what's the bad news?" "Why", says Willie, "I'm afraid your name's on next week's team".

"The Usual, Bella!"

CROWN COURT

I was in this shop the other day. Two old dears were discussing the increases in sweet prices. One says, "By Maggie it's a disgrace putting the price of the bullets up. The only bit pleasure the bairns hev. It's a doonright shyem". The second old lady says, "It's ne good ye moaning Lizzie, ye waad vote Labour, waddent ye?" "Divvent be se daft", says Lizzie, "The Labour's got nowt to de with this, it's the Government that's at fault!"

Jimmie Hogg was talking to Geordie Scott in the club. "By, I had a smashing dream last neet. I dreamt I met Lee Trevino on Gosforth Golf Course, *the great Lee Trevino*. He says, 'Hello Mr. Hogg, would you like to play golf with me?' and there I was playing with the great Lee Trevino". "That's funny", says Geordie Scott, "I had a dream last neet. I dreamt three gorgeous maidens entered my room. They said I was the most handsome man in the world, and began kissing and caressing me". "Ye mean ye had three lovely girls te yersel", says Jimmie Hogg. "Why didn't ye giv iz a ring?" "Oh I did", says Geordie Scott, "But ye were playing golf at the time".

I was in the Doctor's the other day, this fellow says, "Doctor, can I have some more sleeping pills for the wife?" "Certainly!" says the Doctor, "Is she not very well?" "Oh, she's alreet", says the bloke, "The thing is she's wakened up".

Why I meets the same fellow a few weeks later. "How's the wife?" I asked him. "Oh, I've got her a grand job", he says, "She's a lollipop woman at Brands Hatch".

Talking about the Doctor, I said to him one day; "Doctor I waken up every morning laughing at something funny". "Try wearing pyjamas", said the doctor.

I saw this big funeral the other day, about 200 mourners (all men). Behind the hearse was a man with a wonderful Alsatian dog on a lead. I went up to him and said, "Excuse me, sir, is this some civic dignitary or Police Chief who's passed away?" "No", he says, "Actually it's my Mother-in-Law". "Really", I said, "Is that her favourite dog?" "That dog", he said, "Actually killed her, mauled her to death". "You wouldn't like to sell me that dog would you?" I said. He pointed behind him and said "You'll have to join the queue mate".

Aald Billy Wilkie was a Geordie rag and bone scrapman. He passed away and arriving at the Golden Gates, St. Peter met him. "What was your occupation on earth?" he asked Billy. "Scrap man", says Billy. "Wait there!" said Peter, "I'll check up". When he came back Billy had gone. So had the Golden Gates.

"He's a Shift Worker . . .

The mere mention of Work and he Shifts!"

Les Robson saw an advert in the paper: 'HANDYMAN WANTED'. So he went for an interview. "Can you do a bit painting and paper hanging?" said the boss. "No! I'm no good at that", says Les. "What about plumbing and joinery?" said the boss. "Hopeless!" says Les, "I'm nee good at that". "Can you do any electrical work?" says the boss. "Are ye kidding?" says Les. "I thought you were a handyman?" he said. "Why! I just live round the corner", says Les, "Ye couldn't wush for nowt handier than that".

Aald Florrie and aald Bert, both nearing 80 had been walking out together for at least 50 years. One night walking back through the fields after the Bingo session, Florrie says to Bert, "Bert hinnie! D'ye not think it's time ye and me got married?" "Divvent taalk see soft", says Bert, "Whe the hell's ganna marry us at wor age?"

There was a bit trouble with the acoustics in the Catholic Church at Annisford. They set traps for them but it was no avail. So they got two lads from the Rediffusion to put mikes and speakers in the roof. As they were working in the rafters an old lady came into the church and knelt down to pray. Geordie says to his mate, "Switch a mike on and lets have a bit fun". His voice came down the church. "This is the Lord speaking". The old lady never budged. Geordie says, "She must be a bit deaf. Give her the lot, stereo, hi-fi, echo the lot. " His voice boomed down the church, "*This is the Lord speaking*!" The old lady unclasped her hands, looked at the roof and said, "Son, will ye haald yor tongue a minute! I'm trying te taack te yor mithor".

Joe Ridley met Fred Pearson in the club. He says, "Would ye like a pint Fred?" Fred says, "I'll buy them, ye canna afford it, you're working". Joe says, "That's reet Fred. I've got the easiest job I've ivor had, a road sweeper, only two roads to sweep the M.1 and the A.6".

"Ye knaa me missus divvent like understan' me like ye knaa?"
"Frankly, Old Chap neither do I!"

Geordie had just been elected shop steward at Leyland (where you don't clock on you sign the visitor's book). One day he called a meeting. "Lads", he said, "I've got some bad news for ye and some good news. First the bad news. They're ganna reduce wor wages by £2 a week! Now the good news. Ye'll be glad to knaa I fought the gaffers and I've managed to get it back dated two years".

Billy Holmes came hyem one neet laughing all over his fyce. He says to his misses, "What d'ye think pet, I've bought four brand new tyres for the price of two". She says, "I divvent knaa waht ye want wasting yor munny like that for. Buying fower tyres, ye knaa we hevvn't got a car". Billy says, "Alreet, do I complain when ye buy a new brassiere".

"I Telt Her Straight, I'm The Boss!"

A pretty young American school teacher was on loan to a little school in county Durham. First day in class a little boy presented her with a big bunch of flowers. "Excuse me miss, my father sent these for you". (That's the way they taalk in Durham). "Gee son!" she says, "They're just dandy. Thank your pop. Now where can I put these pretty flowers?" One little girl says, "Please miss, put them in the vase". But when she got to the vase it was full of dead flowers. "Jiminy Crackers!" she said, "I jest can't put these fresh flowers among the dead ones. What can I do with the dead flowers?" One laddie says, "Tak them ower the yard, put them in the bin". As she was crossing the yard she met the old caretaker coming out the boilerhouse. "Good morning Mr. Caretaker", she says, "Where's the bin?" "Ah've bin for a smoke hinney", he said, "Where's thou bin?"

Bill Elliot was doing a quiz in the papers when he says to his wife Lizzie, "Where aboots is Nigeria?" "I couldn't say offhand", says Lizzie, "But it can't be far away, cos wor little Willie reckons the Nigerian bairns at his school gaan hyem for their dinner.

Mind the Emperor Hadrian has left his mark in Geordieland here. Look at all the grocer's shops he has, and that great paint factory at Haltwhistle, and furthermore all the Geordie bairns speak fluent Italian. They come hyem from school, open the door and shout, "Mam, am ere!" (MAMA MIA).

I met Sep Walker wearing a brand new suit. "That's a grand suit, Sep", I says, "Do you pick all your own suits or does the wife pick them?" "No Dick", he says, "I pick them mesel, the wife just picks the pockets".

Geordie was at the Labour Exchange. "There's a job here for a bus driver-conductor. Do you think you can manage to drive a bus and take the fares as well?" "Sartinly!" says Geordie, "I'll take the job". The first day he starts the phone rings in the bus depot about 3 p.m. and the inspector picks up the phone—Geordie's on the other end. "This is driver-conductor Broon", he says, "Can ye send help. The bus has mounted the pavement, crashed through a store window, smashing ivverything". "How in the world did that happen?" says the inspector. "I divvent knaa", says Geordie, "I was upstairs taking the fares at the time".

Talking aboot buses, two Geordies coming oot of the dance, teaming of rain. Bill says, "Jim, I doot we've missed the 36 bus hyem and we can't afford a taxi, so it's a waalk hyem in the rain". They were just passing the bus shed when Jim says, "I've got an idea. We'll break in here, nick a bus and get hyem dry. I'll keep a look out while ye gaan in and nick a bus". Why Bill gets in and aboot ten minutes later there's a crashing of glass and rending of torn metal. Jim gets worried.

He looks in and there's dozens of smashed up buses. "What the divils gannin on Bill?" he shoots. Bill says, "The number 36 is reet at the back. I've had to shift aal the others!"

Doris Graham was cleaning her windows standing on the upstairs window sill when she slipped and fell headfirst in the dustbin. Two Chinamen were passing at the time. One Chinaman turned to his mate and says, "Lookee! Englishman velly extlavagant! Woman good for *Years*".

Mind ye get some crackers driving on the roads these days. I was driving along the A.1. when I spotted this old lady at the wheel knitting — actually knitting. I wound my window and shouted at her, "Pull-over!" She smiled at me sweetly and said, "No son! It's a jumper".

When I was a little laddie my dad would say to me, "Dickie, son, if you save your money you'll be a happy successful man in years to come. Now every penny or indeed every shilling you get don't waste it. Put it in that money-box in the cupboard under the staris". Do you knaw, till the day I left home it didn't cost my old man a penny for gas.

Aye he was a clever un, my old man. He says to me, "Dick, the day I die I want you to look in the right hand pocket of that old corduroy jacket hanging on the scullery door. You'll find a one pound note. When my funeral passes the 'Earl Grey' on the High Street, go in and hev yersel a pint and leave me outside, like you always did".

"Divvent take ne notice. He always does this when it's his turn!"

There's these three Irishmen who decided to rob a bank. The plans were all made: Pat drives the getaway car; Mick is the look-out for the police; Shamus is to do the robbery with a suitcase and a sawn off shot-gun. "There's ony one snag", says Shamus, "Me oirish accent when I open me mooth, they'll know I'm oirish and the game will be up". So they sent him to elocution classes in Hazelrigg and after a week he came out talking posh. Eventually the great day came. All went well, the car was ready, Mick was posted to watch. Shamus walked into the bank, morning suit, bowler hat and sawn off shot-gun. He walked to the bank clerk and said, "Look here old man this is a hold up. I want all the money out of the safe. Into this bag, immediately, otherwise I shall have no compunction, I shall be obliged to blow your head clean from your shoulders and I have got just the thing to do it here, a double barrelled sawn off shot-gun!" The bank clerk looked at him and laughed, "You're Irish aren't you?" he said. "How do you know that?" says Shamus. "Ye've sawn the wrong end off the gun", says the clerk.

Mrs. Brown was talking to Mrs. Jones about a visit she had just made to see some of her friends. "De ye mean te say yor friends nivvor asced ye te hev a cup o' tea?" "Why", replied Mrs. Jones, "They nivvor as much as asced me if aa had a mooth!"

"Divvent put it in the Lounge, put it in the Kitchen!"

A miner entered a drapery shop in Byker many years ago. He was asked by the owner as to what he would like and the miner asked to see some 'lang stockin's'. After having had about a dozen pairs to inspect he said that 'nyen o' them wad de for him'. "Well, how's that my good man? These are long enough". "That's aall reet, mistor, but aa want a pair o' bow legged yens".

I was arguing with Geordie Black aboot the Darwin theory, that man was descended from monkies. "For aall ye knaa Dick", he says, "Yor grandfather might have been a great big hairy ape". "It wouldn't worry me", I says, "If me granda was a gorilla". "Mebbe not!" says Geordie, "But I bet it would worry yor grannie".

This Irish lad walked into the pub with two sacks. "They look heavy", I said to him, "What's in them?" "Sure", he said, "They're full of telephones". "What in the divil d'ye want with all of them telephones?" I asks him. "Sure now, it's like this", he says, "Me brother is a great musician and he's formed a dance band. He sent me a letter this morning saying — 'Dear Pat, can you get me two Sax-a-phones'?"

Old Mrs. Proudlock was allocated a new council house after living all her life in an old fashioned colliery row. Two weeks later she ran into her daughter Lizzie in the supermarket. "Hello mother", says Lizzie, "How do you like your new house with all the mod cons?" "Its not bad, hinney", says the old lady, "Only I care nowt for that new fangled weshing machine". "How's that?" says Lizzie. "Why", she says, "Last monday, I put two of your father's shirts and his long hinnings in, pulled the chine, and they disappeared".

Sep Walker was passing the high rise flats in Wallsend with his coal cart when a voice shouted from the window of the 15th floor, "Can I have ten bags please?" To his dismay the lift was out of order so he had to carry them up a bag at a time, up fifteen floors. When he had them in the coalhouse he knocked on the door, said to the lady, "Ten bags of best, hinney, five pounds fifty pence". "I didn't order any coal", she said. "I distinctly heard you order ten bags out the window", says Sep. "I've carried them up fifteen flights". "Good God! It'll hev been wor parrot", she says. So she had to stump up. When her man came in from work he says "Get ready pet, we'll hev a neet at the club". She says, "We've got ne money", and told him about the parrot. He grabs the bird, swung it round and hoyed it in the corner. As he was doing this he tripped over the cat. He gave it a kick and it landed next to the parrot. The parrot opened one eye, looked at the cat and said, "How many bags did you order mate?"

This old Scotsman Jock McKie lives beside me, a real careful Scot. His front door step was worn in the centre. He asked a builder how much it would cost for a new step. "About twenty pounds", said the builder. "Och!" says Jock, "I canna afford that, can you no take the old step oot and reverse it, turn it upside doon?" "Why, I'll try", said the builder. On the day he took out the old step he knocked on Jock's door, "It's ne good, Jock", he says. "I divvent think it's ganna work! Looks like yor father had the same idea before ye".

Geordie was in London outside the Royal Covent Garden Opera House. He said to the commissionaire, "By ye've got a grand place here marra, what neet's de ye hev the bingo?" That's a wonderful northern accent you have sir", said the commissionaire. "Are you an opera lover; for instance do you like Faust and Bach?" "Why Faust's not bad", says Geordie, "And Back's canny, but I canna stand that neet shift".

Tucker entered his leeks in the Club Leek Show. When he got home his wife said, "How did you get on?" "Why", he says, "I won first prize, but I gave it away. It was nee good te me". "What was it?" she asked. "It was a diving suit", he says, "Here's the ticket". She looked at the ticket, "Why ye daft gowk!" she says, "That's not a diving suite, it's a divan suite!"

I went to see one of those 3D films the other day, ye knaa, where everything jumps out of the screen. 'How the West Was Won', they called the picture. There were Indian arrows flying past my head, guns banging in my earholes. I got fed up and said to the fellow sitting next to me, "I've had enough of this, how aboot you and me nipping out for a drink?" "I'd shore like to, pardner", he said, "But I'm in the picture".

Tom the plumber was a hard working man. He would go out to work day or night, whenever he was called on, except one night each year, when he went to the 'Plumbers Annual Dinner'. Well it was on this very night that the phone rang. "Dr. Wright here, can you come and fix my toilet cistern, please, it's leaking?" "I'm sorry doctor, as you know I'd only be too glad, but I'm all dressed up to go oot, my one night off in the year". "Look, I'm your doctor, have I ever refused to come to you when you're ill Tom?" So Tom, dressed in dinner suit and dicky-bow, went round to Dr. Wright's house, marched straight up to the toilet and opened his bag of tools. He took out two asprins, put them in the bowl and pulled the chain and said, "There now, if it isn't any better in the morning call me again".

NORTHUMBRIAN CARDS

These fine postcards are in full colour, Their size varies but most are jumbo size. 120 titles are in preparation, The following are now ready.

(1) "*Durham: South-West Prospect*". Painting by R. Embleton, based on a print. *c.*1770.
(2) "*Alnwick, Market Place*". Water colour based on an engraving by W. Davison, 1826.
(3) "*Warkworth*". Oil painting by unknown artist. *c.*1850.
(4) "*Rothbury c.*1850". Water colour by R. Embleton,
(5) "*Bamburgh c.*1960". Water colour by R. Embleton,
(6) "*Durham Cathedral*". North Side from Framwellgate *c.*1840. Painting by R. Embleton.
(7) "*Holy Island Castle*". Aquatint by W. Daniell, 1822.
(8) "*Hexham Railway Station in* 1832". Painting by R. Embleton, after J. W. Carmichael.
(9) "*Map of Northumberland*". By C. Saxton, 1579.
(10) "*Durham*". Oil painting by J. W. Carmichael.
(11) "*Washington Hall*". Painting by Jim Page.
(12) "*Red-breasted Merganser*". Male and Female. Winters on Holy Island. Painting by R. Embleton.
(13) "*Map of Durham*". By C. Saxton, 1579.
(14) "*Panoramic View of Newcastle*". By Joseph Skelton, 1893.

Price 7p

The following Geordie books are now available

LARN YERSEL GEORDIE by Scott Dobson **50p**
GEORDIE LIFE OF JESUS by Rev. Andrew Elliott .. **35p**
THE GEORDIE BIBLE by Rev. Andrew Elliott **40p**
100 GEORDIE JOKES by Dick Irwin **45p**
THE GEORDIE JOKE BOOK **45p**

GEORDIE SONG BOOKS

TYNESIDE SONGSTER **60p**
GEORDIE RIDLEY SINGS THE BLAYDON RACES .. **60p**
JOE WILSON SINGS **60p**
SONGS OF NORTHUMBRIA by Denis Weatherly
(*all songs have full music score*) **70p**
COME YE NOT FROM NEWCASTLE
A collection of folk songs by Gaven Polevarth
All songs with music **60p**
THE GEORDIE SONG BOOK **50p**

THE GEORDIE COOK BOOK by Peggy Howey **50p**

Also now available the two classic novels of Tyneside life at the beginning of the 20th century.

KIDDAR'S LUCK AND THE AMPERSAND
by Jack Common, ... **£3·75**

GEORDIE PRIDE GREETING CARDS

These magnificent local greeting cards are in full colour and printed on a fine art board. Inside is a description of the painting and the following incription "*with Best Wishes*". By adding appropriate words the cards can be used for every occasion, We have in preparation approximately 100 titles of which twenty two are already on sale. All the cards are from original paintings, many painted expressly for this purpose. The following are now ready:

(1) "*Northumbrian Fisherman*". *c.*1850. Background Holy Island. Painting: R. Embleton,
(2) "*Northumbrian Piper*". Background: Wallington Hall. Painting: R. Embleton.
(3) "*Cushie Butterfield*". Background: Sandgate, Newcastle. Painting: R. Embleton.
(4) "*The Sword Dancers*". Background: Tanfield Rectory Gates. Painting: R. Embleton after R. Hedley.
(5) "*The Knife Grinder*". Background: Percy Street, Newcastle. Painting: R. Embleton.
(6) "*The Keelmen*". Background: Newcastle Quayside. Painting: R. Embleton.
(7) "*The Coachman*". Background: Angel Inn, Corbridge. Painting: R. Embleton.
(8) "*The Cullercoats Fish Wife*". Background: Cullercoats Bay. Painting: R. Embleton.
(9) "*The Side, Newcastle*". Painting: T. M. Richardson.
(10) "*Locomotion No.* 1 *racing coach at opening of Stockton-Darlington Railway*". Painting: R. Embleton.
(11) "*Puffing Billy outside Stephenson's Cottage, Wylam*". Painting: R. Embleton.
(12) "*Locomotion No.* 1". Painting: J. Wigston.
(13) "*Miner's Gala, Durham*". 1872. Painting: R. Embleton.
(14) "*Codex Amiatinus*". Illustrated page from the Jarrow-Monkwearmouth Bible.
(15) "*Roman Army Approaching Vindolanda*". Painting: R. Embleton.
(16) "*Newcastle upon Tyne from St. Anne's Church*". 1835. Painting: J. W. Carmichael.
(17) "*Holy Island*". Oil painting by James Webb. *c.*1860.
(18) "*The Pitman. Outside the Cock Tavern at Durham*". Painting: R. Embleton.
(19) "*Durham*". Oil painting by J. W. Carmichael.
(20) "*Durham: South-West Prospect*". Painting by R. Embleton based on print *c.*1770.
(21) "*Blaydon Races. Leaving Balmbra's*". 1862. Water colour by R. Embleton.
(22) "*The Bigg Market, Newcastle*". Oil painting by Thos. H. Hair, 1875.

The cards are approximately nine inches by six inches.

Price **16p** (inclusive of V.A.T.).